Strategic Business Development

A Practical Guide

Rodolfo Leitón

Copyright © 2023 Rodolfo Leitón

All rights reserved.

ISBN: 9798850135188

Cover artwork by Rodolfo Leitón

DEDICATION

To those who work with the intent of improving other's lives.

CONTENTS

	Acknowledgments	i
1	About This Guide	1
2	Organizational Culture	Pg #8
3	Strategy	Pg #20
4	People	Pg #25
5	Boundaries	Pg #34
6	Sales	Pg #40
7	Growth Management	Pg #47
8	Technology	Pg #55
9	Relationships and Influence	Pg #64
10	A final Word	Pg #74
	Appendix I	Pg #78
	Appendix II	Pg #79
	Appendix III	Pg #85

ACKNOWLEDGMENTS

My wife Elke and sons, Emiliano and Amadeo, have always supported my writing and made it much more enjoyable through their witty criticism. They have joined me many times for literary related activities, and I thank them for their companionship and patience.

Two of my professors from the University of Arkansas became mentors first and then good friends: the late Dr. James A. Millar and Dr. Donald D. White (who also helped edit this book), and to them I owe a debt of gratitude for the positive impact they have had in my life, both personal and professional.

Finally, I would like to thank all those people with whom I have done business over the years for I have learned something from all.

1. ABOUT THIS GUIDE

Why is this guide so simple?

Strategic Business Development (SBD) is composed of strategy, sales, marketing, operations, finance, and organizational culture, among others. SBD requires both science and art. For example, you can use Artificial Intelligence to help you automate processes and make better decisions, but you also need to have people skills and be able to develop relationships with the people with whom you are dealing. It is not a sequential, but rather a synchronous process where many initiatives happen at once. As such, SBD can be quite complicated and difficult to execute if not approached carefully and systematically.

The best way to deal with complexity is to try and simplify as much as possible so a few impactful decisions and actions may be implemented. Focusing on a few key initiatives, and executing them well, provides much better results than trying to work on many fronts at the same time. Lack of focus generally dilutes efforts and wastes valuable resources such as our time and attention.

So, this guide strives to be as simple and straightforward as possible.

Presenting the concept of Strategic Business Development can be a challenge. As Leonardo Da Vinci was alleged to have said, "simplicity is the ultimate sophistication". In other words, it is necessary to the extent possible to simplify complex topics. This guide is concise and to the point and will provide you with what I believe are the main components of Strategic Business Development in very short chapters and plain language.

The components include:

- Organizational Culture
- Strategy
- People
- Boundaries
- Sales and Marketing
- Growth Management
- Technology
- Relationships and Influence

This guide includes concepts I have learned through decades of developing business, organizations, and strategies. The book reflects my successes as well as the mistakes from which I have learned. Developing business is a beautiful undertaking, because it can involve many different disciplines and benefit many people.

This guide does not pretend to be all inclusive and complete. You will be able to add and adjust each section according to your organization's particular situation.

Finally, this guide is for anyone who wants to see their organizations grow and develop into the future. From small entrepreneurs to members of large multinational organizations. For profit business and non-profit entities alike.

For example, non-profit entities need its donors to continue contributing financial and other resources so they may continue their good work. Universities need to continually develop new programs that will elicit a steady "output" of capable graduates that will contribute to society. Every entity, whether it is for profit or not, needs to develop "business" in some way or the other.

We all need to plan our growth into the future and execute that plan, so we may progress. That is how we endure.

What is Strategic Business Development?

If you ask different people "what is Strategic Business Development?", they are likely to provide a variety of responses to your question.

To some, Business Development simply means selling more of their products or services. To others, it may mean integrating other functions like market research, product development, and customer care into the equation. Regardless of who you ask, most people associate SBD with commercial functions.

 **Strategic Business Development is much more than Sales and Marketing.**

I think Strategic Business Development is difficult for some people to understand because too often they attempt to do so in terms of "it's parts" rather than the whole.

Viewing SBD from a single point of view or one's own narrow

experiences leads to a partial, incomplete understanding of what Strategic Business Development really is. This *distortion* reminds me of an ancient parable...

The parable of blind men describing an elephant originated in the Indian subcontinent centuries ago. Each man describes what he perceives to be an elephant after touching a different part of the animal.

One touching a leg thinks it looks like a tree. Another touches a tusk and thinks it looks like is a spear. One feels its side and says it resembles a wall. They all are trying to describe the same animal but do so very differently according to their own experience and unique perceptions.

Blind men and the elephant, 1907 American illustration.

That often is what happens with Strategic Business Development. We try to understand it, but rarely look at it completely. Without comprehending all its parts and how they relate to each other, it is very difficult to know the whole.

The Time Issue

This guide concentrates on long term (Strategic) Business Development and takes a "forest" view of the process. We will not look closely at the "trees", meaning that processes and objectives will be described in general terms.

For example, we will not delve into the short term (Tactics) considerations of generating sales. That includes topics like how to perform market research or develop a sales plan. Nor will we focus on areas like Sales Forecasting and other micro commercial activities which are explained in detail in other books.

Do not expect a detailed "how to guide", but rather a general description of how a Strategic Business Development effort may be built from the ground up. My goal is that after reading this practical guide you will be able to map the path for your organization's own strategic process and have an idea of the major aspects of Strategic Business Development that need to be addressed.

2. ORGANIZATIONAL CULTURE

Organizational Culture is the foundation of Strategic Business Development. Yet, Culture is seldom mentioned as an important ingredient in the long-term growth, capability-building recipe.

This omission occurs because we typically associate Business Development with Sales, Marketing, and other "hard" concepts that can be easily measured and linked to growth. For example, you can objectively measure growth in terms of revenue or new customers. Culture, on the other hand, is a "soft" concept that many organizations do not constantly analyze but it can and should be measured.

Typically, Organizational Culture is treated differently depending on the size of the company. At most small and medium sized entities, you are likely to find someone who is responsible for Sales and Marketing. But you may not find someone who is responsible for Culture. It is just too soft of a concept (perhaps thought to be "unimportant") to have someone be responsible for it, especially when there is so much workload to distribute among a small group of people.

Culture and its impact too often are not understood. As such, it is not given the import and focus that areas like Sales and Marketing do receive. That is a shame, because the right Culture can make companies do wonderful things.

Larger companies, on the other hand, usually place more importance on Organizational Culture and have traditionally asked the Human Resources area to look after the "Culture stuff". In recent years, some organizations have focused more and more on strengthening culture to boost their performance and have gone on to create Chief Culture Officer positions and corresponding support structures.

What is Culture?

Culture is the energy that makes an organization move in a certain direction. It's its fuel. And nothing is more important than Culture when it comes to the long-term performance of a company. Not even Strategy.

That is why, perhaps, the following mis-quote has persisted over time: "Culture eats Strategy for breakfast".

Why is Culture more powerful than Strategy? Because Culture guides decision making and actions inside the organization, which are the key enablers of strategy execution.

Culture often causes us to behave and work in a certain way, and guides people in thinking, acting, and deciding, whether top management realizes it or not.

The best organizations recognize the power of Culture and try to harness it. Especially the ones that want to do sound Strategic Business Development!

Organizational Culture provides us with very important

frameworks for our daily activities:
- What is acceptable in our organization?
- What is not acceptable in our organization?
- How we "do things" in our organization?
- How to decide, in case of doubt.

Peter Drucker has been credited with saying "Culture eats Strategy for Breakfast". The Drucker Institute, however, clarifies that what he said is "Culture—no matter how defined—is singularly persistent."
Photography courtesy of the Drucker Institute.

Culture's Effect on Business Development

I was lucky to be exposed to a strong organizational culture that promoted Business Development at a young age. My first job after Graduate School was as an Assistant Buyer at Walmart International, based in the Bentonville, Arkansas, Home Office.

At the time, Walmart International had stores in Argentina, Brazil, Canada, México, among others. Each country was at a very different stage of its development: Canada and México were the oldest international operations and so had more mature processes in place, while other countries like Germany or Indonesia were struggling to find their place in the Walmart world.

Sometimes the corporate jet had empty seats that needed to be filled. Since most of the trip would be focused on visiting stores, buyers were welcome (and expected) to join. I would volunteer as often as I could, and this gave me the opportunity to travel with some of the very executives I had read about during my MBA studies. For a business nerd like me, this was like traveling with your favorite celebrities!

I was extremely lucky to go on trips with two titans of retail, David Glass and Bobby Martin, then CEO of Walmart Stores, Inc., and CEO of Walmart International respectively.

Getting on those jets, with that team, was an incredible experience. There was a camaraderie and excitement that is difficult to describe, and it was based on all of us being "merchants". It was as if we were all going on a business safari, trying to find growth opportunities. We visited the market, always looking for great products or displays we could replicate in our own stores. It was like a treasure hunt.

Bobby was so focused on visiting competition, that once in Brazil the store manager for French retailer Carrefour welcomed him with a sign: "Welcome Bobby Martin (President of Walmart) to Carrefour". The culture at Walmart was, and I think still is, all about being great merchants and driving sales.

Bobby Martin, then CEO of Walmart International, was known for visiting competitors. He would even get welcome signs (this one from French retailer Carrefour in Brazil).

I recently interviewed Bobby (he is the current Chair of the Board for The Gap, Inc.) for one of the management classes I teach and asked him about the role of the leader in creating a culture of business development. Bobby told me: "Culture is so defining… Culture is the first brick that goes in the wall."

 **"Culture is the first brick that goes in the wall." – Bobby Martin**

The first brick that goes in the wall. That very much sums up the importance of Culture.

Walmart's strong organizational culture originated from its founder, Sam Walton, who was a strong promoter of culture as an enabler of improved organizational performance.

Creating a Company Culture

Once you recognize the importance of Culture to your organization, it's time to work on it. The first step is to have a clear idea of what you want your Culture to be like. In the company that I run, we decided we wanted the Culture to be dominated by our Values, which include Respect, Integrity, Excellence, Service, and Commitment.

How do these Values translate to practice? At our company, we think of them as Values in Action. While envisioning what we want the company culture to be like, we think of it as a place where people give and get Respect. It's an environment where they can argue and discuss, for the betterment of the organization, in a way that is respectful. We also think of our company as one in which Integrity is at the center of everything we think and do. No business result is worth compromising your Integrity. Anyone who does so will be immediately dismissed from our company. We also think of our organization as a place where people do things with Excellence, to the point where team members do not tolerate mediocrity. Our company is one in which our team members strive to Serve their internal and external customers because we know we owe our jobs to them. At the same time, our people truly are Committed to our organization.

If you notice, describing your values in action creates a mental imagery of what your Organizational Culture will be like. So:
1. Determine your Values.
2. Describe your Values in Action.
3. This will describe what your Organizational Culture will be like in real life.

 **Values in Action = Organizational Culture**

Beliefs

Beliefs are important in any company, and they can be used to support your Values and strengthen Organizational Culture.

When thinking about creating a culture that promotes Strategic Business Development, these are some beliefs that we like to reinforce:

- Growth is fun.
- Growth must be profitable.
- Growth makes opportunities for all of us.

Beliefs can also promote the behaviors that are expected of team members. For example, in our organization we strive to be agile (a way of working) and nimble (proactiveness towards challenges and opportunities).

We promote the Belief that we need to do things with efficiency and effectiveness. And that bureaucracy is bad for our company.

Going back to the Walmart example, Sam Walton would always remind his associates (as employees are called at Walmart), that all leaders must be "Servant Leaders". Servant leadership as a belief is very powerful, because it directs people's attention to the fact that people in positions of power have the distinct responsibility to serve others so they may succeed and achieve.

That cultural outcome will be very different from that of a company culture where bosses expect to be served and where the understanding is "we are not all in this together".

"It's more important than ever that we develop leaders who are servants, who listen to their partners—their associates—in a way that creates wonderful morale to help the whole team accomplish an overall goal." Sam Walton, founder of Walmart Stores, Inc. Photo courtesy of the Walmart Museum.

Communication

Once you know what your Values and Beliefs are, you need to get them ingrained in team members' minds. This is not an easy task, and it requires constant repetition.

Our Company Values and Beliefs are reinforced in meetings, office signage, and especially during new-hire onboarding processes. We use storytelling whenever possible to reinforce them. For instance, when someone has gone above and beyond what is expected of them in order to exceed a customer's expectation, we share their story as an example of demonstrating Commitment to our organization's goals.

We also talk about our Values and Beliefs with people outside our organization. For example, when we are evaluating a new business partner, we state our Values clearly when first introducing our company to them. We communicate in clear terms that we will prefer not to do business with partners who do not respect our Values. The sincere act of potentially turning business away for the sake of our Values has a powerful effect on our people. They feel energized and protected because they know what to expect from our company, always.

Being clear about what we will, or will not, do for business has generated respect and credibility with potential business partners. Ironically, the willingness to lose business to protect our Values has generated business for us.

Taking Care of People Strengthens your Culture

We have also defined that, in addition to a Culture anchored by our Values, we want to work in a place that promotes balanced living.

When the Covid-19 pandemic came, we were one of the first companies to implement work from home in our industry. After the pandemic ended, we decided to maintain a hybrid model where our collaborators can work from home and from the office, with most days at the office as a rule.

Taking care of your people goes beyond providing some home office days. You must "put your money where your mouth is". We pay above market wages, and continually check each key team members' compensation package against market studies by reputable consulting firms. In addition to paying well, we have implemented a few programs that make us a desirable place to work.

Becoming a Desirable Employer

You want the right people to want to work with you. And the way to become a desirable employer for these potential hires requires action on different fronts.

First, ensure your work environment is attractive.

Independent audits are useful in determining your actual work environment. Management should not present a version of what it means to work at your company that differs from what team members experience in real life. There are many options available to audit your organization's work environment.

A proper audit or certification process will help identify weak spots in your organizational culture, allowing you to take corrective action. For example, one of our executives was mistreating people to get the results we wanted. We found out because this made us fail a certification process. We fixed this, and other problems, and improved our culture until we were certified.

Second, make sure your people are "taken care of". Because we live in a Third World country and a high percentage of people live in poverty, we wanted to ensure our employee's families were living well. So, we also implemented Oxford University's Multi-Dimensional Poverty Index at our company. The index helped us understand the needs that some of our employees have (such as having a disabled child at home or living in an area where no internet access is available) so we could help them in a more effective way. Knowing how many employees live in harsh conditions, and helping them live better, has become a great opportunity for us.

The combination of strong Company Values that guide everything we do, the conscious effort to constantly strengthen our work environment, and the extra-mile effort of understanding how we can best support our people, have created a powerful mix. Our employees feel motivated, committed, and they want to stay. It is not uncommon for competitors to offer them higher salaries and almost always they decide to stay with us. Our Culture and sense of belonging are that strong. Of course, we have lots of room for improvement, but we are working on it.

Educating your workforce

Education is the key to better jobs and higher salaries. It is also the foundation of a more competitive labor force within your organization, so it makes complete sense to look after your employees' education. We regularly motivate employees to continue their education, whether it is completing their high school diploma, starting undergraduate college studies, or earning an MBA. We back this effort with our money. We offer to pay 50% of the education if certain requirements, like good grades, are met.

The fact that we actively support our people's education has created a sense of belonging and appreciation towards the organization where everybody wins.

More education leads to better salaries, which in turn lead to better quality of living for our employees and their loved ones. At the same time the organization benefits from a better educated workforce that generates improved results.

Having a committed, loyal workforce can result from a simple process that may be hard to execute. Rooted in a strong organizational culture, make sure your work environment is attractive, your employees are "taken care of" and that you help develop them by supporting their education.

Now that we have discussed Organizational Culture and its importance for behaviors, decision making, and actions, we can move on to discuss strategy.

The link between Organizational Culture and Strategy is:

 **Culture is the Compass.
Strategy is the Map.**

The Appendix includes some questions that may help you in the process of defining and strengthening your Organizational Culture.

3. STRATEGY

Once you have defined what you want your Organizational Culture to be like, and how to reinforce it continually, you will have defined a framework for how the people in your organization generally should:

1. Behave
2. Decide
3. Act

In other words, your "execution-mindset" is ready.

How People Behave, Decide and Act
=
Execution Mindset

Following the Culture/Strategy order, now that you are clear about how you will go about working, you must decide what it is you want to achieve. So, Strategy comes next.

There are many ways to understand the term Strategy. Merriam-Webster dictionary defines strategy as "a careful plan"[i]. In his article titled "What is Strategy?", Michael Porter states that Strategy is, in essence, "choosing to do things differently than competitors do" and to carefully decide what to do and what not to do[ii]. In other words, to have focus.

We will not dive into how to create a strategy in this guide, because there is ample material available on the subject, and I do not have much to offer in this regard.

My intention, as was stated earlier in this guide is to focus instead on Strategic Business Development. My one suggestion relative to communicating a Strategy is as follows: Keep it simple. Concise and clear is much better than extended and convoluted. Complex does not equal Smart.

Many times, strategic plans are constructed in long formats, with many pages of content that make their communication and comprehension to most team members complicated. Interminable jargon and illustrations may impede understanding of the organization's priorities.

"Now if you turn to page 136, that's when things really start to get interesting."

Source: Living the Strategy, Paul Niven & Tor Inge Vasshus.
Cartoon by Jonathan Brown, used with permission from Corporater.

Obviously, it is important to go through all the analysis and discussion necessary to produce a solid strategic plan. That part needs to happen, and it needs to be thorough and complete. But when the final product is created, when the organization's strategy is finished, the sensible thing to do is to present it simply.

It's like eating sausage. You know what it is, you want to enjoy it in a hot dog, but you do not necessarily want to know its ingredients.

For this reason, I believe the presentation and communication of strategic plans should always be concise. A "One Pager" format is preferable. This may seem too simple, too "light", but having your Strategy summed up in a concise manner can enable execution by making it more accessible to everyone involved.

The One Pager should include:

- <u>Values.</u> What are the Values that will guide decision making and actions? Integrity, Excellence, Service are often used, among others, and are necessary choices in a growing organization.
- <u>Vision.</u> How do you visualize your organization in the future?
- <u>Mission.</u> Why does your organization exist?
- <u>Building Blocks.</u> What are the key initiatives that will enable you to execute your strategy well? How much will they contribute? For example, launching a new product line may add incremental business for X amount of dollars.
- <u>Differentiators.</u> What makes your organization different? Why would your customers value your company more

than your competitors?

- <u>Pillars.</u> What are the key strategic areas of your business. For example, our Strategic Plan has "Operational Excellence" as one of our Pillars. We limit Pillars to five to maintain focus and simplicity.
- <u>Objectives.</u> What are the objectives for each of your Pillars? For example, for Operational Excellence one of our Objectives is to "Use efficiency as a growth engine".
- <u>Priorities.</u> What are the key initiatives your organization needs to execute to achieve your objectives? For our company to achieve Operational Excellence, for example, our priorities include "inventory optimization".
- <u>Key Performance Indicators.</u> How will you measure progress in achieving your Priorities? For example, for Inventory optimization our Key Performance Indicators include "Days of Inventory" (how many days it would take for us to sell all our inventory, at the current rate of sale).

The key consideration about your Strategic Plan, however you develop it, is that it is easily understandable to everyone in your team. The priorities need to be clear, precise, and easy to remember. Key Performance Indicators should be numerical and simple to measure, so they remain objective and executable.

Sometimes managers think sophisticated indicators are best. The moment those indicators become so complex that only a few people in the organization understand how they are measured, you lose their value because we generally do not commit to what we cannot understand. If most people in the organization do not understand how your chosen indicator is determined (for example share price) whatever commitment your people offer will be weak.

 **We Generally Do Not Commit to What We Cannot Understand.**

Many companies keep the Strategic Plan visible only to top management and it is seldom discussed. I would recommend that you display yours in large traffic areas of your company. Everyone should know what your organization's strategic plan states, and you should periodically review your progress for each of the Pillars with your organization's middle management and operational leadership.

The reason I prefer the Strategy One Pager is that is makes the Strategic Plan simple to understand and more accessible.

The Appendix at the end of the guide includes a template for a Strategy One Pager that may be helpful in creating your own, as well as some instructions on how to complete it.

4. PEOPLE

After defining a Culture and Strategy that are conducive to Strategic Business Development, we need to work defining what group of people will do the work. The suggested steps are:

1. Know Your Current Team.
2. Design Your Ideal Team.
3. Build Your New Team.

Know Your Current Team

Let's begin with knowing your current Team. You may say "I already know them". Perhaps you know their names, where they are from, their educational background, and how dependable they are, for example. But do you know how they think?

This is important, because when you add up the thinking styles of your most important team members you end up with their collective thinking style. Your organization's performance is a result of the sum of everyone's decision making, interpretations of information, and actions which are all based on thinking. This is why you need to understand how your key people think collectively, or what I call your Team's Brain.

Collective leadership thinking = Team Brain

A popular method of identifying people's way of thinking is the brain quadrant method, which is derived from Carl Jung's theories. Today, there are several methodologies available to test people and determine their thinking style. These methodologies include DISC, Herrmann and Benzinger, among others. Nevertheless, they all share some basic characteristics:

- The brain is divided into four sections or quadrants.
- Testing identifies a person's dominant quadrant based on the way they think.
- People are then classified according to their thinking style (what they prefer, how they process information or how they react to stress, for example).

The brain quadrant method states that the dominance of a quadrant determines a person's type of thinking, way of perceiving the environment, and processing information:

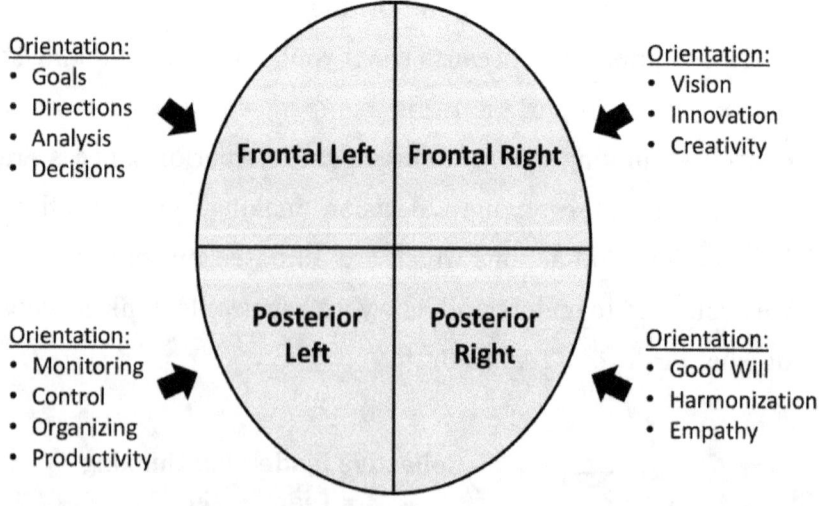

So, every person will have a distinct way of thinking based on which quadrant is more dominant in their case.

When thinking about your Team Brain, they key is to understand how team members may complement each other, so that they possess the right capabilities to execute the strategy.

***

There are limitations to the "brain quadrant" methodology. Categorizing thinking patterns is difficult and can lead to mistakes in perception. As Psychology Today[iii] states:

"Like many ways of categorizing people, the left brain / right brain dichotomy is appealing, promising to teach individuals about how they think and why. But the reality of hemispheric specialization is much more complex than this popular concept suggests."

Therefore, while there are limitations and risks in the use of this methodology, "Brain Mapping" does serve as one way to understand team member's ways of thinking and how they could complement each other. In other words, it can help us better understand our Team Brain.

Brain Mapping refers to the simple act of locating everyone's results on a single brain drawing and evaluating where your people fall. Let me give you an example. At our company, when we mapped our team members' thinking styles, we found something interesting.

Without realizing it, I had created a leadership team that overcompensated my weaknesses. Let me explain: my thinking style test results state that I am a "Front Right Quadrant" person. The report says I am "visionary, creative and a risk taker", and that

I like to focus on "inventing and experimenting". But, as my family may correctly point out, I am also unstructured and very disorganized. It understandably drives them crazy that I am so scattered.

While I was building our team, I was constantly looking for people who could complement my weaknesses. I searched for structured and organized professionals who could contribute to making our growing business great at **controlled execution.**

Because of mistakes I made years ago, I know how important it is for me to surround myself with team members who are very structured, analytic, process-oriented and objective. In other words, people who think in a way that is the opposite of how I think.

That led me to hiring mostly "Left Brain" people for leadership positions, and I went too far:

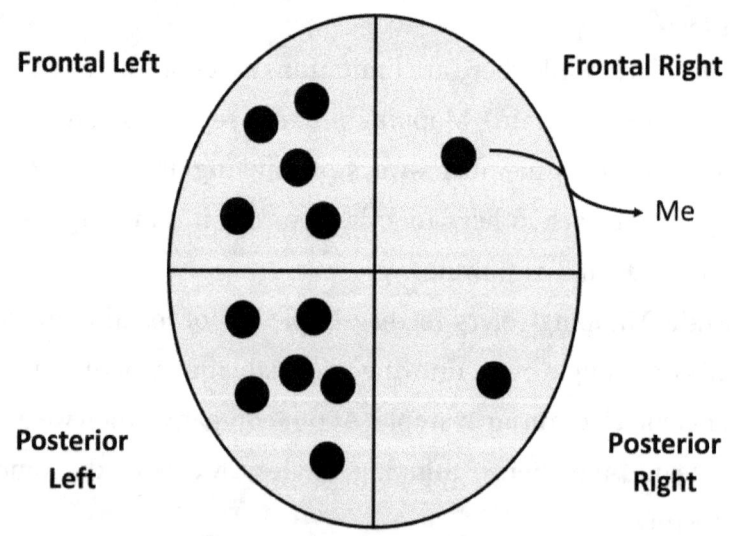

Clearly, I built a Team Brain that was unbalanced and with too few "Right Brain" leaders, and this needed to be corrected.

Design Your Ideal Team

Once you know your team better, it is time to think of how to raise its level. How do you create your Ideal Team?

Mapping our team's thinking style as well as my own enabled me to see my mistake and correct it. Now we have hired more "Right Brain" team members to help us balance our thinking style and take our company into new areas of growth. We still have a majority of "Left Brain" leaders in our organization because in our business gross profit margins are slim, and having tight control of working capital is essential to our profitability. Inventory and accounts receivable is where a large portion of our working capital are allocated, and properly forecasting inventories and managing customer's payments requires a very controlled and methodical approach that is best carried out by "Left Brain" team members.

Advertising companies, for example, may need more "Right Brain" people that are creative and inventive. An aerospace engineering firm, on the other hand, may benefit more from having more "Left Brain" team members, such as mechanical or electrical engineers. All companies need all quadrants, the question is how to allocate your Team Brain according to your organization's needs.

There is no one recipe for every company. There is not a "right and wrong" way to populate your Team Brain. Having the right balance does not mean your organization should have a 50/50 Left/Right balance.

The right balance is the one that gives your organization the type of talent required to achieve its goals.

What matters is that you understand how your Team Brain is currently made up, evaluate against what you think your desired composition should be, and then take appropriate action.

Get/Develop/Keep

To keep your Strategic Business Development initiatives running at full speed you will need to continually fine tune your team. This means your Human Resource Department should be focused on three key areas related to People:

- Get. Job descriptions and position profiles for jobs that are related to Business Development need to be reviewed to make sure you are recruiting the right types of candidates needed for business development. Leadership positions should continually be on the lookout for great talent that could make an impact in your organization. Hire them whenever possible. If you do not have a vacant position for great talent, find one. Fire someone else if needed to make room (more on that later).
- Develop. Talent can be hired, but it should also be developed. Always try to hire from within, make it a point to offer newly available positions to your current team members. This will create an atmosphere where people will work hard because they know if they deliver results, they can grow. If no one qualifies, then hire from outside. Identify team members with potential to grow and give them the tools to succeed. Help pay for their education, provide them with courses or seminars to continue

developing their knowledge or skills, and be an active proponent of people development. This will do wonders for your Strategic Business Development. Finally, your organization should have a "Talent Development Plan" to ensure you will have talent who can effectively manage future complexities and grow profitably.

- <u>Keep.</u> Pay top money to top performers. When a competitor tries to hire your talent away from your organization, try to keep them. Spend a little more if you must. Keeping top talent in a growing organization is key. And remember that not all compensation is nominal. Having a strong and positive organizational culture can make people turn down higher salary offers from your competitors. Because many will rather stay in a company they love, rather than make more money somewhere else. (I love it when one of our team members rejects a competitor because they prefer working with us.)

"Smart, Fun People that Can Execute"

Giora Kaplan is a founder of Israel-based Wix.com, a cloud-based development platform that has rapidly grown since its foundation in 2006. Part of Wix's growth success is that they have created a very simple recipe for driving business development through their team members. They do this by working hard to ensure they have "Smart, Fun people that can Execute".

Wix has a methodical assessment of employees where they are classified into **A** and **B**. **A's** are the ones that "if you lose them, you are risking the business... that if you go away for six months when you come back your business is better off than when you went away".

B employees are trained, taught, and supported so they can grow. A and B employees are well compensated and taken care of. Kaplan says companies should "Fire Quickly", meaning that they should replace anyone who is not an A or a B employee.

While Kaplan's methodology may neglect people development (for those who are neither an A or a B employee), if you aspire to develop an organization that focuses on delivering excellence and quality, a filtering method that allows you to retain and empower high achievers and reliable workers is necessary.

Keeping mediocre team members is bad for the organization, bad for performance, and bad for overall morale. Having a methodology that allows your organization to organically focus on developing and strengthening good performers while replacing bad ones is essential to profitable Strategic Business Development.

Build Your New Team

When designing your New Team, ask yourself the following questions:
1. How would I describe my Ideal Team in one sentence?
2. What would be the top three attributes of this team?
3. If I mapped the Ideal Team's brain, what would it look like?
4. Which three Key Performance Indicators would you use to evaluate whether your Ideal Team is successful or not?

This exercise is best when performed by key leaders in your organization, along with their direct reports.

***

Values, Values, Values

In addition to understanding how your key team members think, and how they could complement each other at work, I would like to stress again the importance of having your people:

1. **Align Their Actions with Your Organizational Values.** For example, if Integrity is one of your organization's Values and you find out your best salesperson has cheated to make her numbers, you should dismiss her immediately. The organization's Values are sacred.

2. **Believe in your Mission and Vision.** Your team members must believe in your company's reason for existence and have a common view of the future.

3. **Remain committed to the Strategy.** Having key team members deviate from the charted course only makes the organization go slower and possibly make costly mistakes. They must stick to the program. A sound strategy exists to be followed. The strategy may be periodically re-evalued, but while it is valid it must be followed!

5. BOUNDARIES

Business Development requires clear boundaries that force the organization to have even more focus. These limits must be placed on several fronts, including the following: Behavioral, Financial, Logistical and Strategic.

Behavioral

Mark Van Der Weerden is a long time executive at French consumer goods company Bic. They make ballpoint pens, lighters, and shaving razors and pride themselves on the quality and practical design of their products.

Mark has had a successful career developing business for the company at very different locations such as Russia, Bulgaria, France, Guatemala, and Dubai, to name a few. He has been very effective in very different cultures and is a disciple of Fons Trompenaars in his understanding of cultural differences.

But Mark has some common "tools" he uses with his business partners, regardless of where they come from. When meeting them Mark is tough but fair. Always very decisive and focused. And his customers love his approach.

I was at a sales convention organized by his team, and it caught my attention that the closing slide during the main event's presentation was titled "Behaviors for Success" and included the following bullet points (bold text is as the original):

- **"Understand that this is a journey**, and this is not a quick fix.
- **We need collaborators** to contribute towards problem resolution – Shift mindset from "their problem" to "our problem". #ONEBIC
- **Our customer** is our number 1 priority! Ensure our actions and solutions are guided with the customer in mind.
- **Focus on what matters** – Focus on the things that make a difference (80/20 rule).
- **Make decisions faster** – don't wait for 100% of information, data is ever changing. Make informative decisions and adjust as new information evolves.
- **Drive continuous improvement** – Constantly find ways to do things better or simpler, don't wait for processes to break. Bring ideas and solutions!"

In one simple slide Mark was telling his sales and supply chain teams, as well as Bic's customers, how the organization expects them to behave, and problem solve, in their joint pursuit of business development. This is important because Bic operates in the consumer goods industry, which is known for tight schedules, aggressive sales goals, and a lot of pressure to make your numbers.

The opportunity for adversarial relationships that may impede sales growth is ample. Setting boundaries to help the teams avoid those traps is key.

Setting boundaries for how we expect our teams to behave when developing business is a very important tool in that it allows people to work with a clear understanding of what is expected of them as well as what to expect of its counterparts in the process.

Financial

It may seem obvious, but many companies do not set financial boundaries to their business development efforts and end up getting into financial trouble for that mistake.

I remember the case of a Brazilian manufacturer who got a first order with an U.S. customer. The factory's owner was very excited because this new business meant their entrance into that very important market. Very soon, before the first year of business was over, this entrepreneur had ordered new machinery to increase his production capacity. In his mind, he was getting ready for tremendous growth from new products and new customers that would surely follow his first U.S. deal.

Unfortunately, the products did not sell that well and were not included in the customer's purchase plan for the following year. The customer informed the manufacturer well in advance, following their mutual written agreement correctly, that they would not be buying more inventories once they had fulfilled their commitments.

The manufacturer panicked. They had just taken significant loans to purchase new machinery and increase their production capacity. How would they pay for all this if their customer in the United States was not going to buy anymore?

It was a mistake on the manufacturer's part to leverage their company so prematurely. They were able to survive by ultimately substituting that volume with other customers in Europe, but before that they went through a painful and difficult time which included laying off employees, negotiating with their lenders, and reducing their operation.

Setting financial boundaries to Business Development is key. Going back to the basics, your budgeting process should allow for business development initiatives, which should be paid for with your current level of business. Do not make the mistake of budgeting aggressive sales increases that may or may not happen.

The cost and risk of new business opportunities should be covered by your current level of business.

Do not leverage your company with the hopes that your new business development opportunities will pay for that leverage.

In addition to budgeting your business development initiatives, you should have a process to help you decide whether a project is potentially viable or not. Building a Business Case for each opportunity will help you in the process.

Here are some considerations for an initiative's Business Case:

- <u>Strategic Fit.</u> Is the initiative aligned with your long-term strategy? Are you remaining focused on what your organization decided beforehand would be the areas that should interest you?

- <u>Projected Profit and Loss.</u> Develop an estimated profit and loss statement for the project. Are you being realistic about expected revenue? Are you being overly optimistic? Are you certain that total costs are included? Make sure to have every department that would be involved in the project review expected costs.
- <u>Cost of Opportunity.</u> When reviewing the project's viability, determine what is your cost of opportunity for not doing the project. Will passing on this opportunity hinder your future, or would it be irrelevant?

Logistical

My day-to-day work is overseeing a consumer goods company. We are focused on selling three distinct types of product: dry food, personal care products, and cleaning supplies. This means our supply chain is "dry", or non-refrigerated. Therefore, we have a logistical restriction in terms of what we can sell to our customers.

We regularly receive offers to distribute products that do not fit our supply chain capabilities. Some of these opportunities I would love to take on such as ice cream, frozen meals, and vaccines, for example. While there are great opportunities in these categories (who doesn't love ice cream?), acting on those opportunities would create major problems for our company.

For example, we would need to invest in frozen storage and transportation or find a third-party logistics provider since our current infrastructure does not allow for this type of merchandise. Since our goal is to drive as much volume through our current system, thereby generating economies of scale and more profitability, the project would not generate any synergies.

On paper you can make any opportunity look good. But in our case a major factor in maintaining good efficiency and profitability levels depends on "saying no" to anything that deviates from our strategy and current business model.

This approach is not for everyone. Some organizations have ample resources to try and test new ventures that take them outside of their current business model. In our case, resources are limited, and we must be very disciplined about how we use our logistics infrastructure.

 **Any business opportunity can look good on paper.**

Strategic

The reason so many strategies fail is that many companies lose focus and lack the discipline to execute them. There are always exciting new opportunities that can make us lose focus. As Michael Porter said, strategy requires you to choose what *not* to do.

So, simply put, strategy is also meant to act as a boundary to help you stay focused. Do not make the mistake of deviating from your strategy just because a shiny new opportunity comes up. You need to consider and evaluate it, of course, but always be mindful of the fact that in the past you made a commitment to follow a certain path through your strategy, and some opportunities may cause you to lose your way.

6. SALES

As mentioned at the beginning of this Guide, many people confuse Business Development with growing revenue, but a long-term growth effort requires much more. In this section, we will cover the basic strategic areas that need to be considered to grow sales.

Again, we will not delve into tactical processes such as how to define a sales budget or how to manage a marketing team. We will focus only on the structural aspects of Strategic Business Development, no matter how basic they may seem.

The Fundamentals

I believe the most basic concepts are sometimes the most powerful ones. That is why we begin this section on sales with one of the simplest, yet most insightful approaches to getting your sales fundamentals in place: the Four P's (Price, Product, Placement, Promotion), which were popularized in the 1960's book "Basic Marketing: A Managerial Approach" by E. Jerome McCarthy.

Since its publication, the concept has evolved to include additional factors, but since we are tackling those same topics in other parts of this book, and because I think generally the original is always better in its simplicity, we will only cover McCarthy's four (McCarthy, 1960, 45-47)[iv] which include the Customer at the center.

At first glance one may think that these principles apply only to companies that sell products. But these principles apply to any type of organization, including those that sell services and non-profit entities which are required to raise donations to fund their operations. Think of the Consumer as the person, company, or organization with which you need to increase productive dealings with when using this methodology to help you develop business.

McCarthy argues we should place the Consumer at the center of our efforts and do so in the following areas:

- **Product:** Do we have the right product for our customers? Think of Kodak, which went from market leader to bankruptcy for basically not offering the right product at the right time. After decades of successfully selling film photography, Kodak failed to adjust when the consumer moved to digital photography and ended up losing market value. Ironically Kodak invented a digital camera before its competitors but did not act on the opportunity. Having the right Product is key.

- **Place:** Do we offer the right product at the right location? Would a new luxury watch priced at $12,000 fit well in a closeout store that is visited mostly by people looking for bargains? Does it make sense to go ask for donations to the unemployment office? Probably not. Right Placement is key.

- **Price:** Do we have the right price for our customer? Consumers may shift brand preferences if the price is not right for them. For example, car company Hyundai has been able to grow its market share by gaining customers thanks to its competitive prices and good quality. Your goods and services must be priced correctly if you expect to generate revenue.

- **Promotion:** are we making it exciting, attractive, for the consumer to buy our product? There are many ways to do this: discounts, digital marketing, and endorsements to name a few. We will discuss more on this topic when we cover Influence. You must Promote Correctly.

Having the right Product, at the right Place, at the right Price, with the right Promotion will be conducive to increasing revenue. Again, this applies to all industries: services, pharmaceutical, apparel, technology, personal care, food, etc.

You can more appropriately work on other areas of your business development once you have a clearer understanding of the Four P's fundamentals of your product or service.

Key Sales Initiatives

To structure your long-term sales growth plan, you will need to focus on the following areas:

1. **Market research:** Your organization should do market research to identify potential markets, competitors, and consumer trends whether you are a non-profit competing for donor funds, or a tech company launching a great app.
2. **Lead generation and customer retention:** How do you identify potential donors to help your non-profit? Who are your potential customers? How do you retain new customers?
3. **Commercial:** Your sales and marketing departments should develop strategies to promote your product or service. How do you stand out from the competition? How do you communicate to your customer what makes your product or service different from the rest?
4. **Training and development:** Are your people trained in how to sell your product or service? Do they know the industry and competitors? Have they been trained in negotiation techniques? Do they know how to deal with rejection? Do they have grit?
5. **Product development:** Is your organization developing the products and services that customers will require in the future? Do you have a clear pipeline of products and services that will help you grow year after

year? Is it aligned with your strategy? How are new product launches prioritized? What will their Return on Investment be?

Don't Chase Sales

Chasing sales is one of the costliest mistakes you can make. This often happens when you see other organizations doing great in a particular field of business and you want to participate.

Being able to capture a new rising opportunity, without chasing sales, should only occur when you have:

1. The right timing. Your organization is poised to take advantage of the opportunity at an early stage.
2. The right resources. Your organization has the right resources to take advantage of the opportunity.
3. A solid exit strategy. If things do not work out, your organization can exit the opportunity "unharmed".

Chasing sales may cause your organization to suffer some of the following:

a) Bad investments in infrastructure or machinery.
b) Excess inventories due to unrealized demand.
c) Loss of focus that leads to more lost sales.

The Covid-19 pandemic can provide an excellent example. Because the medical profession recommended using hand sanitizer to stop the spread of the coronavirus, product sales quickly skyrocketed, giving way to shortages and price increases. Those companies that *already were* in the hand sanitizer business, saw strong sales and profits coming from this product almost overnight. It became a great business to be in.

Soon, many other organizations also wanted a piece of the hand sanitizer market. While companies that already sold the product ramped up production, those that wanted to get in rushed to get other manufacturers to make it for them. Retailers developed private label versions. Even companies who were in the sugar and distillery business found a way to launch their own hand sanitizer.

And then, as often happens, demand started to cool off while new supply began to become widely available.

To the horror of companies who had just invested in hand sanitizer inventories, supply outstripped demand and prices fell precipitously.

When demand cooled off and new supply hit the market, companies found themselves with huge excess inventories. Some offered 4x1 (buy one, get four) to get rid of the inventory. "It's worth more to us gone", some said.
From the Wall Street Journal, May 20th, 2021.

This dynamic of chasing sales, only to find yourself later wishing you had never invested in the opportunity, is common. It happens in all industries.

Jeff Bezos, founder of Amazon, said it best[v]: "never chase the hot thing, whatever it is. That's like trying to catch the wave. You'll never catch it. You need to position yourself and wait for the wave and the way you do that is you pick something you're passionate about."

There is a big difference between strategically focusing on how to grow your business, so you can take advantage of the right opportunities and being an opportunist. Don't simply be an opportunist. Be strategic about how you will grow your business.

Therefore, in Strategic Business Development keep in mind these best practices to avoid chasing sales:

1. Be clear about how you want to grow.
2. Be disciplined about following your strategy.
3. Resist fads.

 **Don't Be an Opportunist.**

7. GROWTH MANAGEMENT

Managing the growth of your organization helps ensure long term development. The best approach to managing growth is a gradual, steady, and incremental process. This process needs to be based in a solid, well thought out plan.

Think of it as building a house. Your home should be built on top of a solid foundation if it is to endure time and weather.

Laying a foundation on poor soil will only weaken the foundation, and a house built on a weak foundation is bound to collapse when placed under stress. Think of houses that collapse during an earthquake, while many other houses around them remain unaffected by the tremor.

A house built on a solid foundation will endure and resist more when placed under stress.

The same happens with growth management, which acts as an important tool of Strategic Business Development. If you have a solid growth management plan in place, you will be able to better:

1. Identify those opportunities that you should take, and

those that you should not take.

2. Allocate resources in a manner consistent with your financial limitations and strategy.
3. Plan how to execute the opportunity more profitably.
4. Devise an exit plan in case the opportunity fails to materialize, and you need to limit your losses.

Growth Is Not the Objective

I have seen many companies or divisions within companies, start to grow too quickly and only to find themselves suddenly going out of business. What happened? They did not manage their growth.

Many confuse growth's objective in organizations, as an end in itself. Growth for growth's sake is detrimental because it takes focus from what really matters: creating value for the customer.

Whether it is helping people learn how to read at a non-profit, opening another bakery, or launching a new product line, your organization should always understand growth as a medium to generate value for your customers and other stakeholders.

Managing growth requires that you consider:

- Growth Methodology
- Focus on Profitability
- Organizational Design

 **Creating Value, not Growth, is the Objective!**

Growth Methodology

Deciding how to approach growth efforts is critical, because growing in an unplanned manner can have very negative effects for your organization. On the other hand, having a pre-planned growth method is good for your organization because:

1. It will help you focus.
2. It will make you more resilient when facing failures.
3. It will give you limits.

One of the best books for understanding Growth Methodology is Ram Charam's "Profitable Growth". Using a baseball simile, Charam says that when thinking about how to grow organizations sometimes focus too much on "hitting" home runs.

This focus could translate, for example, into a company betting all its future growth on a single product line. If the product line fails and the company had nothing else to fall back on, at best there will be no growth, and at worst it's future could be compromised. Similarly, relying too much on a single customer, no matter how large or attractive, could have a devastating impact should the customer find another supplier or simply decided to no longer do business with the organization.

Home runs are hard to get, and it is risky to bet all your growth into home runs and then striking out. It is safer and more productive to try to get some hits.

If an organization diversifies its risk by having smaller and diverse initiatives, there is a higher probability that if several of them fail these setbacks will not hinder potential growth too much. At the same time, if just a couple of these smaller initiatives do work, then you could potentially have tremendous upside.

In Strategic Business Development you should always strive to diversify risk. Do not bet your future on hitting a "home run".

About the Pipeline

An important part of Growth Management is managing your "pipeline" of new products, businesses, or other initiatives that will contribute to future revenue and profit growth.

By pipeline I mean a series of assorted:

1. New revenue generators.
2. New profit generators.
3. New efficiency generators.

New revenue generators are those initiatives that may result in **sales increases** and typically come in the form of new product launches, new categories, or areas of business, or new divisions altogether.

Profit generators are those initiatives that may help your organization improve **profit margins** and this includes everything from reducing product or service costs to increasing profit margins through price management.

And efficiency generators will be those initiatives that allow your organization to be more, well, efficient. That means **doing more with less**.

Creating a pipeline of said initiatives is quite simple, you just need to sit down with other team members and write down whatever actions you think may assist you in promoting sales increases, improving profit margins, and controlling/reducing operating costs. Then, prioritize them and keep the top three for each of the areas. You can always add more once you have successfully achieved the initial ones.

Strategic Business Development

As stated in the previous section, risk management is key: you want to diversify your pipeline so that if your plans work or do not work, you can adjust your total plans.

Using another simile, think of it as going saltwater fishing on a trolling boat. Typically, you will have several rods fixed to different parts of the boat, and each rod will have a particular lure according to what you are hoping to fish. Each line may have a different length and may be fitted with different weights to that the lures are moving at different depths.

This combination of different lures, fishing line length, bait depth, and angle at which they are presented create a distinct fishing opportunity. Some may catch a Marlin, some may catch a Mahi Mahi, while others may catch an old rubber boot.

The same is true for your Strategic Business Development pipeline: if you pursue different alternatives, diversify by placing numerous well thought out "bets", and are persistent, you may create some outstanding opportunities for growth.

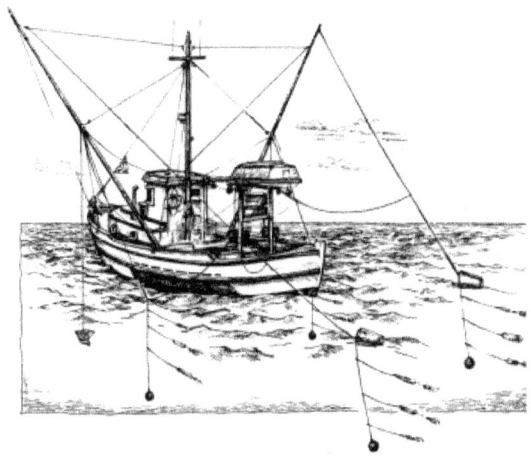

Salmon Trolling Boat. Courtesy Alaska Trollers Association.

Focus On Profitability

Unless you are like Elon Musk and have billions of dollars to bet on turning a profit "someday in the future", don't pursue money-losing ventures with the *hope* they will someday pay off. It rarely happens.

Be conservative when making financial projections.

It is common, in all types and sizes of organizations, to make the mistake of "falling in love with the project". People too often become so excited about a new product or service, that they fail to adequately assess the risks associated with the opportunity.

My recommendation is that when making financial projections for a new business development opportunity you:

1. <u>Be Realistic When Projecting Sales.</u> Be conservative when estimating income, no matter how "hot" the opportunity is.

2. <u>Lowball your profit margins.</u> Something will always happen that ends up eroding some of the initially estimated profit margin. It could be higher logistics costs, changes in raw material or services costs, exchange rate fluctuations, etc. Don't be surprised by profitability that is lower than planned.

3. <u>Monitor your planned costs.</u> Did you consider all the personnel that will be needed to successfully achieve your objectives? The financial cost of working capital, or the maintenance cost on new machinery? Have you included all potential costs? Or are you planning so that your project seems feasible and gets approved?

 ## Be Conservative When Making Financial Projections

Organizational Design

Organizational Design is the process of creating the structure and processes that enable the operation to achieve its goals.

In a small bakery, for example, organizational design may mean defining workers' tasks around the basic functions of baking bread and taking care of customers at the cash register.

For larger organizations, Organizational Design may require re-defining organizational charts, creating new processes, promoting a substantive change in how the labor force is structured, and defining whether certain tasks should be exported to other geographies.

Not only does Organizational Design aid the process of getting the job done, but it can also be a liberating force that allows companies to grow.

Take the example of Sergio Paiz, of Guatemalan conglomerate PDC. With operations in various Latin American countries, PDC is involved in consumer goods manufacturing and distribution services, both for their own brands and other global brands.

After the sudden death of his father, Paiz found himself in charge of a large group of companies that were operating in an uncoordinated manner. This left ample opportunity for better cooperation among the parts, and for generating efficiencies and efficacies.

Paiz sold some businesses, focused on others, and ultimately sought help to re-design their organization. With the assistance of organizational expert Dean Meyer, PDC undertook an Organizational Design exercise which would completely transform their culture, organizational chart, and way of working in general.

The transformation process was well planned, and design principles were clearly documented. The principle-based design of the new organization was, in fact, the easy part. For Paiz, the most difficult part of the re-design was changing the team's composition: "A challenge for me was resisting the temptation to compromise the structure to accommodate people. In fact, the hardest part of my job was letting go the people who needed to leave and recruiting the right talent. This has taken a few years. It was personally painful, and drained huge amounts of my energy. But it was the right thing to do, really the only thing to do."

The new Organizational Design proved to be an enabler of Business Development. According to Paiz, "the new structure has been an engine for our growth."

PDC has sustained 30 percent growth in EBITA year over year for the last decade, because of their new Organizational Design and complementing changes.

 **Organizational Design is a valuable tool in Strategic Business Development.**

8. TECHNOLOGY

In today's environment, all organizations should have the right tools to help them run their operations so that they may act with:

- <u>Agility.</u> Organizations must be responsive to their constituents needs and adjust nimbly to changing market conditions.
- <u>Efficiency.</u> Getting the job correctly with as little cost as possible.
- <u>Control.</u> The quickest way to lose money is by not controlling the operation effectively.

The main strategic technical enabler for a growing organization is the Enterprise Resource Planning system, or ERP. An ERP is a software system that allows you to run your business while integrating different functions such as sales, finance, operations, supply chain, and other areas. It is the information, process, and control backbone of an organization.

World class ERPs now include Artificial Intelligence to help your organization navigate business more efficiently, for example by aiding users and suggesting process improvements.

Quality systems are available to companies of all sizes: leading providers such as Oracle, SAP and Microsoft do offer scaled down

ERP versions for small organizations. It is worth your while to investigate available options and to adopt one that is made by a reputable and experienced company.

Organizations should choose carefully when deciding on an ERP. Some are best suited to commercial companies while others are best for logistics ones. Gartner Incorporated publishes an annual ERP quadrant rating by industry, company size and location, that may serve as a guide. Here is a sample of how they classify the leading ERPs:

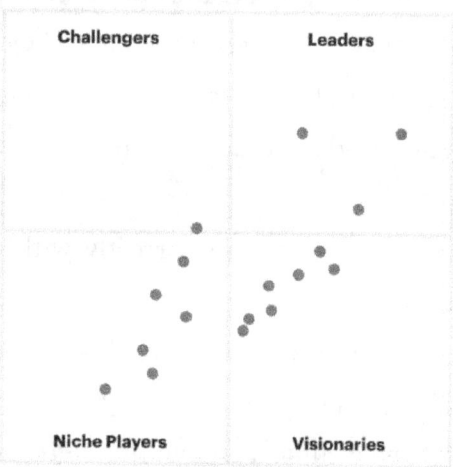

A simple, inexpensive way to get an idea of which ERP might be good for your organization is to look at your more competitors. Which ERP are the most successful competitors using? Try and talk to people in your organization's ecosystem and find out the pros and cons of the various options that they implemented. You might be surprised at how much information colleagues and even competitors are willing to share if you show a willingness to reciprocate.

ERP Costs

When selecting an ERP, be careful to consider its Total Cost of Implementation. Here are some examples of costs you need to consider when evaluating your investment:

- **Cost of ERP licenses.** This means the cost of paying your ERP provider for the use of its system. Nowadays most providers sell a subscription, which means your organization does not actually buy the ERP. Instead, you sign a long-term contract which stipulates a monthly fee for the use of the system. The more users, the more licenses you will pay.

- **Integration costs.** If you have other systems that need to be connected to your ERP, they all need to communicate to ensure your operation runs smoothly. For example, in our organization we receive orders in various ways. Consumer online orders flow directly into the ERP, while large retailers send their orders through "Electronic Data Interchange" and need to be fed into the ERP through a systems integration. Integrating other systems into your new ERP will take time and money.

- **Consulting costs.** When implementing a new ERP, your organization will likely need guidance in the process. For startups it may mean one or two people giving you advice, while for large organizations it may mean dozens of people split up into functional areas such as Master Data, Supply Chain, Finance, etc. Always look for consultants who have relevant experience and a successful track record in your field of work when hiring.

Poor advice when implementing an ERP can bring untold sorrow and spiraling costs to your organization.

- **People costs.** In mid to large size ERP implementations, your organization will be asked to provide several personnel to work exclusively on the project. This may include top executives, mid-level managers, and even some operations personnel. Taking these people out of your day-to-day activities will have several associated costs including the cost of replacing them as well as the efficiencies that are lost while the new hires learn the ropes. Nevertheless, the quality of those people you provide will impact the quality of the ERP you end up implementing.
- **Customization costs.** Current ERPs come with the benefit of Global best practices integrated into them in every area. Finance, Human Resources, Operations, all offer the best of what your ERP provider has learned over the years and from its many customers around the World. Aside from mandatory adjustments that are required to comply with local laws, you should refrain from customizing your new ERP for two reasons:
    - **Cost:** Each change will require hours of programming that will be billed at a high hourly consultant's rate. The more complex your request, the more expensive it will be. The more changes you make to the ERP, the higher your consulting fees. Be wary of "scope creep", which happens when your project expands beyond its

original goals, causing costly delays.
- **Risk.** Your new ERP was created as an integrated solution. Every time you make changes to the original version you create potential integration problems. The more changes you request, the higher the risk of the system not working correctly when you start to use it.

These are some, but not all, of the costs that make up your Total Cost of Implementation. Be sure to know the estimated <u>total cost</u> when approving the budget!

Selecting your ERP

Here are some suggested steps in the selection process:

1. <u>Define the Team.</u> From the beginning, a group of supporters must be created. This group of supporters must include the organizations' leader (the CEO, or the Divisional Vice President, for example). Don't bother advancing with an ERP project if your organization's leader is not on board. He or she should be your biggest supporter.
2. <u>Agree on the Need.</u> Get internal agreement about the need to find a new ERP, and why your organization needs it.
3. <u>Set the Budget.</u> Implementing an ERP is a significant investment. You definitively should have a budget because implementations can easily become much more expensive than you thought possible at first. Define how much it is you are willing to invest and stick to the budget.

4. <u>Think of the Future.</u> Make the most out of your ERP investment. Think ten years ahead: how do you visualize your company? Whether it is going from one fast food franchise to five or expanding your financial services business to other continents, thinking of the future when selecting your new ERP is of great value because you will be better positioned to take on later opportunities.

Save Money, Avoid Pain

ERP implementations can be costly and painful. There are many cases of companies losing shareholder value, and facing intense financial crises, due to bad ERP implementations. ERP implementations are not to be taken lightly.

Here are some basic suggestions to help you steer away from ERP implementation trouble:

1. <u>Seek Good Guidance.</u> Whether you are responsible for a mom-and-pop store, or a multinational operation, seeking the right help and guidance in implementing your ERP is key. Make sure whoever you consider has the right experience in implementing systems in your industry. Figure out if they expect to do mostly remote (bad) or on-site (good) work. Tie over 50% of the implementation's consultants' fees tied to the latter parts of the project (especially the testing and "Go Live" stages).

2. <u>Eliminate Saboteurs.</u> The ERP implementation can help your organization grow and develop business into the future. It is of the utmost importance the implementation is successful. There are many things that can go wrong, and the last thing you need is anyone in your organization

(especially top executives) sabotaging the effort. Sabotage can be discreet and private, but it is always easy to identify: lack of commitment by those who are part of the project, reflected in missing key meetings, constantly complaining about the process, and not doing quality work for the project are some telling signs. If you see a saboteur, tell them to get on board and really support the ERP implementation. If they don't quickly change, change them for someone else. And use the experience to show everyone else that saboteurs will not be tolerated. Be careful too with "outside saboteurs", meaning people that are not part of the project or that were taken out of the project. Research by Donald D. White and David Bednar[vi] show these saboteurs may cause as much distraction and damage from the outside as they could from inside the project.

3. <u>Pursue the Standard.</u> Your new ERP will increase your implementation costs through consulting programming hours and increase the risk that systems will not work as intended because you are changing them. Resist the temptation. Go with the standard solution as much as you can.

4. <u>Mind the Data.</u> Master Data is all the information that goes into the ERP. This includes product descriptions, price lists, employee names, etc. Some ERP systems will not work properly if the information that goes into them is incorrect. For example, a bar code that has one digit missing is considered faulty Master Data. This defect may cause the system not to work until the information is fixed. Faulty Master Data has caused havoc among some of the largest

corporations in the World. For example, when Target Stores launched their new Canadian operation faulty information was partly to blame for the retailer's spectacular initial failure and for that operation going out of business soon afterwards[vii]. Typically, ERP providers write into their contracts that the responsibility for the quality of Master Data rests with the customer (you). It's in your best interest to make sure your Master Data is clean, correct, and relevant.

Artificial Intelligence

Artificial Intelligence (AI) will surely have an enormous impact on Strategic Business Development. At the time of this writing, AI is being used by several organizations to perform certain tactical (short term) business development functions. For example:

- Sales.
- Advertising.
- Customer Service.
- Tactical negotiations.

By tactical negotiations I mean repetitive, high-volume agreements typical of certain industries. Companies have started using AI to help them deal with these negotiations and optimize resources in the short term, but also with an eye for freeing time so that human negotiators can focus on the long term. "Instead of replacing human employees, we are eliminating the mundane, low-input aspects of a procurement executive's job, freeing up time for strategic negotiations"[viii], says Martin Rand, CEO of Pactum, a firm that develops AI aided negotiation systems. AI can facilitate tactical and repetitive negotiations faster and more objectively than a person can.

For **Strategic** Business Development, at the time of this writing, AI has limited participation in long term processes that require:

a) Multi organization, multi stakeholder coordination.
b) Synchronous execution.
c) Long term, multifaceted efforts.
d) Different processes and systems that currently are driven by long term decision making.
e) The human relational aspect of the process.

Nevertheless, the technology is evolving fast, and we should expect AI should have a more complex and strategic influence on SBD in the future.

We may even benefit from AI acting in the long-term relational aspect of Strategic Business Development.

Eventually, AI entities will probably develop mutually beneficial, long term, business relationships with humans and themselves on behalf of their organizations.

"One must not compel nature but persuade her". - Epicurus

9. RELATIONSHIPS & INFLUENCE

For what seemed like an eternity, our company could not get a certain large customer to buy from us. This was a significant challenge because they represented a very important sales opportunity for some of our products.

No matter how hard we tried, we would always get turned down. But one day, things changed and soon we were developing more and more business. I knew the reason was that we hired a new salesperson who knew these customers for a long time, but I wanted to see for myself. So, I jumped on a plane to visit the customer with our team. I wanted to see the dynamic with our new salesperson while he met with several department executives at the customer's headquarters.

Seeing our new salesperson interact with the customer allowed me to confirm he had a great relationship with them. After exchanging pleasantries and moving into business topics there was real camaraderie, even when discussing difficult issues that are normal to every business negotiation, such as what happens with rebates if sales quotas are not met.

Now, I am terrible at telling jokes and small talk. But I do recognize the importance of developing relationships in the process of Strategic Business Development.

Relationships

Building strong relationships requires time and effort. But most importantly, is requires trust. Trust exists when you:

1. Know your counterpart will deal with you in good faith; and,
2. Know what to expect from them.

You will never have a strong relationship with someone you do not trust, or vice versa. Building trust is one of the most important foundations of developing long term relationships for life, and for Strategic Business Development.

Relationships can be built between individuals, and between organizations. With organizations, the distinction is that sometimes the corporate culture is so strong in its Values, that when someone in that organization changes the people in the other organization believe all dealings with this new counterpart will be done in a way consistent with previous dealings.

And that if trouble ensues it will be resolved with a Win-Win mentality. Even if they do not have a trusting personal relationship.

Of course, Credibility also is important to building strong relationships and is different from Trust. Credibility exists when:
1. There is demonstrable knowledge or experience; and
2. There is congruence between what is said and done.

"If you tell the truth, you do not have to remember anything."
– Attributed to Mark Twain. Public domain photograph.

If you can be trusted and you are credible, more, and bigger doors will open in your Strategic Business Development quest. This is not something you can "fake it till you make it". Building trust and credibility require a lot of work and time.

The bottom line here is simple, do everything you can to ensure that trust and credibility are maintained with all your stakeholders. And remember that both are easily lost, so protect your organizational trust and credibility accordingly.

We will not dive into the subject of how to develop relationships, but it is worth noting that investing in teaching your people how to build productive relationships is an important part of your Strategic Business Development process.

Unfortunately, in this era of intensive social media and virtual interactions, many of us have lost the ability to properly exchange ideas in a way that leads to relationship building. Young people, especially those most affected by the social isolation caused by the Covid-19 pandemic, may need help in this regard.

In keeping the focus on the basics, you might investigate material by Dale Carnegie, who wrote extensively on the subject in a way that is easy to understand and implement. Things like "don't criticize", "be an attentive listener" or "remember and call people by their name" should make sense to every person in your organization.

Relationships are the basis for Strategic Business Development, and organizations help their employees understand their importance, as well as how to foster and strengthen said relationships.

Ethics

Strategic Business Development (SBD) should only be pursued as an honest and constructive goal, with the idea of improving the situation of everyone involved. If you are looking to develop business without regard to moral or ethical standards, this guide is not for you.

To help make sure persuasion efforts are ethical, the TARES test was developed by Baker and Martinson in 2001[ix]. The test asks that we review our efforts considering:

1. Truthfulness: if the message we are trying to convey true? Are we making things up to get the result we want?
2. Authenticity: are we being honest in how we present ourselves to those we want to persuade? Or are we making up credentials, for example, to seem more credible?
3. Respect: are we acting with respect for those we seek to influence?
4. Equity: are we being fair and balanced?
5. Social Responsibility: is our proposal harmful to society or the environment?

Before you embark on a new SBD initiative, ask yourself: does this pass the TARES test?

Influence

Influence is key in Strategic Business Development. Any SBD process will require your organization to influence others to establish new relationships, gain new business, obtain financing, and other objectives that are critical to long-term growth. Being able to influence others will greatly improve your chances of developing long term business.

Once you have committed to being ethical about your influencing efforts, you should focus on appropriate influencing techniques. One of the best sources for information on the science and art of influence is Dr. Robert B. Cialdini's classic book "Influence: The Psychology of Persuasion". Besides explaining the science behind how humans may be influenced, Cialdini shares influence methodologies that he calls "Levers of Influence". Here are a few examples:

- <u>Reciprocity.</u> It is in human nature to reciprocate. People feel obliged to return in kind favors, gifts, or services they receive. For example, reciprocity is used by consumer goods companies, by offering a small product sample so a that potential customer may try the product free of charge. Cialdini says the promoter giving away the free sample can "release the natural indebting force inherent in a gift". Many of the people receiving the free sample end up buying the product to "return the favor". So, when trying to influence a counterpart it always helps if you first give something to them first.

- <u>Authority.</u> Imagine an ad where a medical doctor recommends that you smoke. That happened! Between the 1930's and 1950's medical journals ran cigarette ads featuring doctors. Why did the ads work? Because we tend to value an authority's opinion when making decisions, having an expert back up our claims is a powerful tool. And if a doctor says it is O.K. to smoke, it must be, correct? The roman poet Virgil (70 BC – 19 BC) said it best: "Believe an expert." We tend to accept proposals more easily when they are endorsed by an authority we trust. This applies in many fields. Have you seen Dwayne Johnson, a.k.a. "The Rock", promoting exercise apparel?

From Fashionnetwork.com coverage of Under Armour's deal with Dwayne Johnson.

- <u>Scarcity.</u> People often perceive that scarcity equals value. That is why when we see a "only 2 left!" message on the airline ticket we are purchasing online we tend to want to buy it before they are sold out. Scarcity can be a very useful tool to influence others, especially when you have a timeline and need a way to motivate your counterpart to decide.

Visualization

Visualization is a way to influence oneself, and that can be a valuable component of your SBD toolkit, especially when you are facing the inevitable setbacks and challenges that arise. When things are not going well, and you need extra motivation, it is of utmost importance to stay positive. And Visualization can be very helpful in that regard.

There are two ways of Visualizing:

1. The Wrong Way.

2. The Right Way.

The Wrong Way of Visualizing consists of empty repetition and imagery, where people tend to believe that if they want something "badly enough", and that if they truly *believe* they will get what they want, they will.

It is unfortunate to see people not doing any hard work, any real effort, while "manifesting" that their dreams will become a reality just because they declare they will. Or, even worse, because they feel entitled to get what they want.

Lazy, empty repetition and visualization are a waste of time.

The Right Way to Visualize is to combine hard work, determination, and grit, with an objective optimism that you will achieve what you want to achieve.

By Objective Optimism I mean having a realistic belief that you will achieve your goals *if you do the work and things go well*. Doing the work is a must, but sometimes our work is negatively affected by things we cannot control.

Think of all the good, hard-working entrepreneurs that opened a restaurant just before the Covid-19 pandemic. They may have worked hard, wished for the best, but events out of their control ruined their plans. It happens.

 **Hard Work + Grit + Objective Optimism + Visualization = Better Results.**

Ideally, the Visualization process should consist of:
1. Having a realistic vision of what you want to achieve.
2. Seeing that vision just when you awake, and before going to sleep, which is when your subconscious mind is more receptive.
3. Working hard, and smart, every single day to achieve your vision.
4. Not letting problems or other obstacles stop you. Find a way to get things done. But...
5. Know when to stop! Use the boundaries we have discussed in previous sections of this guide to help determine when you need to change focus.

Pygmalion and Galatea. Artist: Jean-Léon Gérôme, Year 1890, Medium: Oil on canvas, Dimensions: 89 cm × 69 cm (35 in × 27 in), Location: Metropolitan Museum of Art, New York City.

This is one of my favorite paintings, because it is related to Visualization and Achievement. The topic is taken from Ovid's Metamorphoses and shows the sculptor Pygmalion, who created a statue of a woman so beautiful that he fell in love with it. Longing for a real woman in the likeness of his statue, he prayed to the goddess Aphrodite to grant him this wish. The painting shows the moment Aphrodite brings Galatea, the statue, to life.

10. A FINAL WORD

Strategic Business Development is not a sequential process. You do not work on Culture first, then on Strategy, then on building your Team, etc. While the ideas in this book are presented in a linear way for clarity and to help you organize, in real life a solid long term business development effort will require your company to work on several initiatives simultaneously.

Strategic Business Development is synchronous, meaning that its processes may happen at the same time rather than starting a process once another is finished.

Once you have clearly defined what your organizational culture should be like, you need to continually reinforce how you want your people to behave, decide and act. Every possible meeting should reinforce the importance of following the Values you have chosen to guide your people. Your organization should post culture-related communications clearly visible at facilities' entrances, meeting rooms, cafeterias, and even the restrooms.

You should also use storytelling to help reinforce desired behaviors and to recognize people who have acted based on your organization's Values. Culture is like a plant that continually needs to be taken care of to become stronger and grow.

"People" is another area that needs to be continually addressed. There always will be opportunities to mold and renew your team. People will retire, move on to other opportunities, or leave for other reasons. You should always be on the lookout for talented potential hires. I like to keep a "Hireable Folder", where I collect resumés of potential hires I think might someday make great team members. Having a "Talent Development Plan" is vital to SBD and a responsibility of your organization's leadership.

The same is true for education. Your people can always learn more, sharpen their skills, and be better qualified to do their jobs. Having a continuous talent development plan is very important, and it should be an important part of your organization's leadership efforts.

Strategy reflects long term thinking, nevertheless it does need to be reviewed and periodically updated. We like to conduct a review every three years, unless a major change in our business requires us to review our strategy before its scheduled time.

All Strategic Business Development's components need to be continually evaluated and changes made when deemed appropriate.

Strategic Business Development is a never-ending process. It requires Science (machine learning, Artificial Intelligence aided forecasting and negotiation, financial structuring, etc.). It also requires focusing on the Art of relationship building, talent development and retention, business acumen, etc. The process is complex and demanding, but it can also be fun and personally rewarding.

And, Strategic Business Development is a process best carried out, to use Stanley A. McChrystal's term, by a "Team of Teams", meaning that the process will require the simultaneous, coordinated work of different functional groups.

As with all daunting tasks, Strategic Business Development should be approached as a challenging and exciting endeavor where your teams are all working towards a noble end… the long-term growth of your organization for the good of all stakeholders.

Strategic Business Development is best when lived stoically. You must be firmly resolved to do what is right for the organization while recognizing that setbacks will inevitably arise.

Finally, Strategic Business Development should be pursued with the intention of improving conditions for the organization's stakeholders. Whether it is providing more aid through your non-profit organization, creating more jobs at your small business, bringing new technologies to underdeveloped countries that will improve people's lives, or creating shareholder value, the growth you seek should have an edifying purpose.

I hope my suggestions are helpful in your quest to grow and expand, and that your initiatives are successful.

Strategic Business Development

Appendix I - Organizational Culture
Questions to Consider

- What are the Values that you want your organization to observe and use daily?
- How would you describe the ideal Organizational Culture at your company or institution?
- What should be person to person, and group to group, interactions like within your organization? Especially when addressing difficult topics?
- Are you, as a leader or person who cares about the organization, an example of its Values?
- How are you measuring what your organization's work environment is like?
- What are you doing to improve the work environment?
- How are you measuring employee well-being?
- What are you doing to improve employee well-being?
- Are you supporting your employees' development by providing them with enough training and by facilitating learning opportunities?
- Are you instilling the mentality that profitable growth is necessary your organization and its people to prosper?

Appendix II - Completing the Strategy One Pager

This Appendix shares some suggestions on how to complete a suggested template for the Strategy One Pager:

Strategy One Pager Template

Values	Mission & Vision	Building Blocks		Differentiators
		Priorities	Key Performance Indicators	
Pillar	**Objective**			
1.		1. 2. 3.	1. 2. 3.	
2.		1. 2. 3.	1. 2. 3.	
3.		1. 2. 3.	1. 2. 3.	
4.		1. 2. 3.	1. 2. 3.	
5.		1. 2. 3.	1. 2. 3.	

Values

Values are the principles that will guide how the people in your organization Decide, Behave, and Act. They are one of the most important components of organizational culture. Please consider:

- What Values should guide our organization?
- Of those Values, which would be the top five?
- Once you have identified those Values, briefly describe them. For example, if you chose Integrity as a Value, then you could consider "we do everything according to the highest ethical standards, always respecting the Law and each other; no business result is more important than our Integrity as an organization and as team members".

Mission

- What is your organization's reason for existence?

Vision

- How do you visualize your organization in 5-10 years?

Building Blocks

Building Blocks are those initiatives that will "boost" your organization's development plans. They may be a new product, service, donor base, or a new business division that will allow the organization to develop business much faster and in greater volume.

Building Blocks may also include initiatives that will improve profitability or efficiency for your organization. Think of implementing a new ERP, reducing inventories so you may liberate working capital, or finding a new source for your raw materials that may increase profit margins.

Differentiators

Differentiators are those aspects of your business that make it stand out. It may be that your non-profit serves an otherwise unsupported part of the disabled population. Or that your coffee shop continually serves uncommon blends from little known growers. Or that your Fintech company provides a service no other competitors can match in your market.

Differentiation is a key component of popular strategy development methodologies like "Blue Ocean Strategy", which was developed by W. Chan Kim and Renée Mauborgne. In Blue Ocean technique, both low cost and differentiation are pursued with the intention of creating new business opportunities.

Differentiators may accelerate SBD, and it is worth your while to identify or develop them as part of your strategic plan.

Pillars

Pillars are those key areas where your strategic work will focus on. They are broadly defined.

Examples of Pillars organizations may use include People, Technology, Operations, and Profitability, and they are thoroughly detailed in the following sections of the Strategy One Pager.

Objective

For each Pillar, you must define the Objective you will accomplish to fulfill your Strategy. For example, for the People Pillar, you may have an objective that your organization is a

Desirable Place to Work for talent (thereby improving the chances high performers will want to join your organization, allowing for better performance and results).

Priorities

What do you need to execute to achieve your Objective. Limit yourself, for focus' sake, to three Priorities. Following the People Pillar example, where your Objective is to become a Desirable Place to Work, you may define priorities such as:

a) Strengthening organizational culture.
b) Develop key talent in the organization.
c) Implement Variable Pay for Performance.

Key Performance Indicators

Finally, you need to measure what you are trying to improve. Following the People Pillar example, and the priorities presented in the previous section, for each priority you need to identify a measurable and objective key performance indicator that will allow you to understand whether you are being successful in achieving your priorities or not:

Priority	Key Performance Indicator
Strengthening organizational culture.	Audit score: Organizational culture and.
Develop key talent in the organization.	Key Talent Rating: 9-Box Method.
Implement Variable Pay for Performance.	Bonus payment tied to numerical achievements.

Creating a Strategy One Pager will be tremendously helpful in communicating your strategy to the whole organization by keeping it simple. Change the One Pager as you see fit, to match your organization's particular needs.

Periodic Reviews and Updates

Strategy requires to be reviewed and periodically updated. To maintain focus, I recommend that all key areas are reviewed monthly. For example:

- Is your organization continually reinforcing its Values, Mission, Vision? How?
- How are you making sure the new hires fit in the organization's culture for business development?
- What does your "talent pipeline" look like? Include both internal development opportunities and potential hires from outside the company.
- Which improvements can be made to your processes and systems to make your commercial processes leaner and more customer friendly?
- What does your Business Development pipeline look like? Any potential new business coming online soon? What are you working on for next five years? Ten years?
- What do you need to prepare (capital, people, infrastructure, etc.) to accommodate this new business well into your existing operation?
- How will new business development opportunities impact your organizational design?
- As you re-design your organization, does your current

talent pool match the new positions and structure?

These are a few examples of considerations you should be addressing on a periodic basis. Each organization is different; work out a list of what makes sense to your SBD plan and be consistent in following progress in those areas and metrics you have identified as important to your long-term growth.

Appendix III - Boundaries

Having well defined Boundaries is key to Strategic Business Development (SBD) to protect your organization's well-being and profitability.

When evaluating SBD initiatives ask yourself:
- Does this opportunity fit into our Strategy?
- Are we generating economies of scale or other efficiencies that will improve profitability?
- Does our organization currently have the resources needed to execute this SBD opportunity? (Human, financial, logistical, technological, etc.)
- If our organization does not have the resources, are they within our current budget or do we have to incur in debt to procure those resources?
- If we proceeded with this SBD opportunity, what is the financial and strategic impact to our organization if the project is a failure?
- Are we being conservative regarding revenue, profit, and costs when estimating the opportunity's Return on Investment?
- Does our organization really need this opportunity for its Strategic Business Development? Or we are just pursuing it because we "like it"?

ABOUT THE AUTHOR

Rodolfo Leitón leads a consumer goods company that operates in Central America, is a member of the University of Arkansas' Walton College of Business' Dean's Alumni Advisory Council, occasionally teaches entrepreneurship courses at the Universidad de Costa Rica, sits on the Board of a retail company, and is a co-founder of Colectivo Empresarial, a non-profit organization that seeks to inform society of the importance and benefits of the private sector.

On his free time, Rodolfo likes to write screenplays and novels. "I Took Panama" is a historical novel based on the life of French Engineer Philippe Bunau-Varilla, the man who helped complete the Panama Canal by convincing the United States Government to stop construction of the Nicaragua Canal and instead complete the Panama Canal, which France started to build but could not complete.

Citations.

[i] Merrian-Webster Dictionary. (2023, June). *Strategy, Noun.* https://www.merriam-webster.com/dictionary/strategy

[ii] Porter, Michael. (1993, November). *What Is Strategy?* Harvard Business Review. https://hbr.org/1996/11/what-is-strategy

[iii] Psychology Today Staff. (2023, June). *Left Brain - Right Brain.* Psychology Today. https://www.psychologytoday.com/us/basics/left-brain-right-brain#left-brained-and-right-brained-people

[iv] E. Jerome McCarthy. *Basic Marketing: A Managerial Approach.* (Richard D. Irwin, 1960), 45-47.

[v] Amazon Web Services. (2012, November). *re:Invent Day 2: Fireside Chat with Jeff Bezos & Werner Vogels.* [Video]. Youtube. https://www.youtube.com/watch?v=O4MtQGRIIuA

[vi] Donald D White and David A Bednar. *"Locating Problems with Quality Circles"* (National Productivity Review, Winter Edition 1984-85), 49.

[vii] Castaldo, Joe. (2016, January). *The Last Days of Target.* Canadian Business. https://archive.canadianbusiness.com/the-last-days-of-target-canada/

[viii] McKendrick, Joe. (2023, May). *Your Next Negotiating Partner: Artificial Intelligence.* Forbes. https://www.forbes.com/sites/joemckendrick/2023/03/17/your-next-negotiating-partner-artificial-intelligence/?sh=8c10705605b8

[ix] Baker S. and Martinson D.L. (2001). *"The TARES Test: Five Principles for Ethical Persuasion"*. Journal of Mass Media Ethics 16, No. 2 & 3: pp. 148-175.

www.ingramcontent.com/pod-product-compliance
Lightning Source LLC
Chambersburg PA
CBHW050247220526
45465CB00002B/589